D1394109

The Wizard of
Id Abra Cadaver!

Johnny Hart and
Brant Parker

CORONET BOOKS
Hodder and Stoughton

Copyright © 1975, 1976 Field Newspaper Syndicate, Inc.

First published in the United States
of America 1983 by Ballantine Books

Coronet edition 1985

British Library C.I.P.

Hart, Johnny
  The Wizard of Id Abra Cadaver!
  I. Title   II. Parker, Brant
  741.5·973   PN6727.H3/

  ISBN 0-340-36700-8

Printed and bound in Great Britain for
Hodder and Stoughton Paperbacks, a
division of Hodder and Stoughton Ltd.,
Mill Road, Dunton Green, Sevenoaks,
Kent (Editorial Office: 47 Bedford
Square, London, WC1 3DP) by
Hunt Barnard Printing Ltd.,
Aylesbury, Bucks.

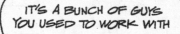

9-1

9-2

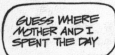

CRASH

9-23

10·1

CREEAKKK

10·6

10-7

CLICK

I'VE NEVER BEEN ABLE TO FIGURE THIS ONE OUT

ME NEITHER

SPLASH

10-29

10-31

12-6

12-17

HI.....I'M
CLAIRE VOYANT...

12:27

I KNEW
YOU WERE
GOING TO
SAY THAT.

ALLOW ME, SIR

12:29

SWISH

ONE SMALL STEP FOR MAN ... ONE GIANT STEP FOR THE ERA.

1-13

2·2

2-12